GREA EXPLORERS

Written by Charlotte Guillain
Illustrated by Jim Mitchell

Contents

Collins

Incredible explorers

People have always wanted to find new places. Great explorers such as Christopher Columbus and Neil Armstrong made dangerous journeys into the unknown.

Christopher Columbus sailed across the Atlantic Ocean in the 15th century in search of new lands. Hundreds of years later, Neil Armstrong travelled into space and was the first human to explore the moon.

Both these men are remembered in history for their discoveries. So, what does it take to be a great explorer?

Christopher Columbus was born around 1450.
He grew up in the **port** of Genoa, in Italy.
At that time, people were starting to travel
further in ships to find new places to **trade** with.
Christopher's father was a **merchant**.
He wanted his son to make lots of money so
he sent Christopher to work on trading ships
when he was just a boy.

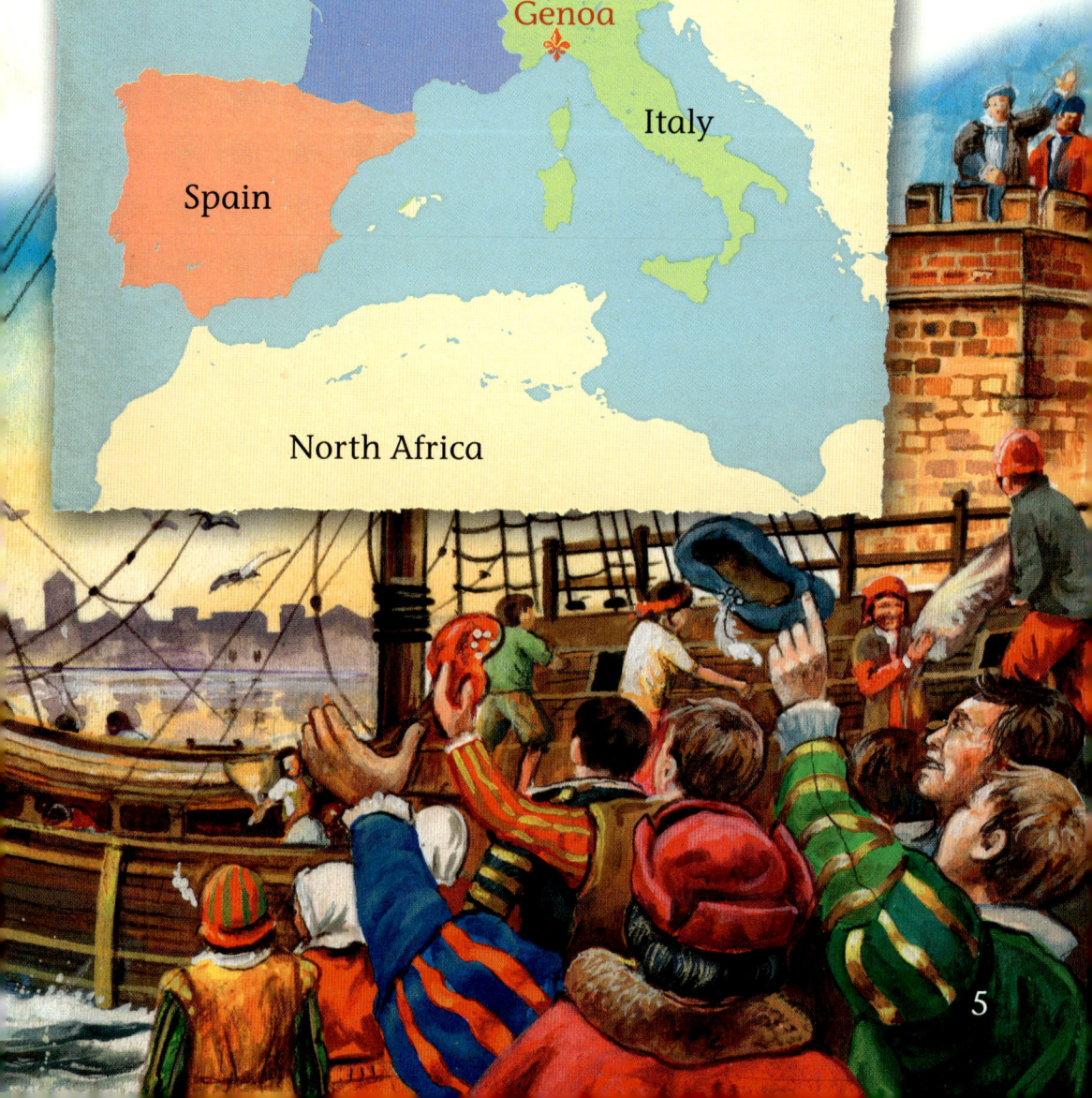

UK

France

Genoa

Italy

Spain

North Africa

Becoming an explorer

Christopher learnt the skills he needed to be a good explorer by sailing around Europe. He **navigated** using the stars and the sun, and he learnt how to use a **compass** and to make maps of new places. He wanted to find a quicker way to sail to Asia to trade and he thought he could do this by sailing west across the Atlantic Ocean.

the journey from Europe across the Atlantic Ocean

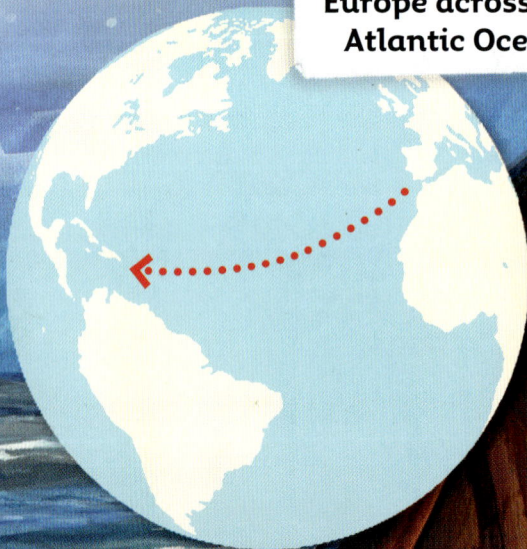

Discovering the Americas

Christopher needed ships for his **voyage**. After many years, King Ferdinand and Queen Isabella of Spain agreed to pay for them as long as Christopher gave any new land and treasure to Spain. He set sail in August 1492 with three ships: the *Santa Maria*, the *Niña* and the *Pinta*.

The voyage was very difficult because the ships got damaged and had to be repaired, and Christopher's compass broke. After 36 days they arrived in the Bahamas, but Christopher still thought it was Asia and named the islands the Indies. Much later, he found out he'd travelled to Central America – somewhere he hadn't known existed until then.

Christopher found peaceful, friendly people living in the Bahamas. He saw they had gold so he took some of them prisoner and made them give him the gold. Then he took some of these prisoners back to Spain. He made three more voyages to the Americas before he died.

Who was Neil Armstrong?

Neil Armstrong was born in 1930 and grew up in Ohio, in the USA. He was very interested in aeroplanes as a boy. He had a **licence** to fly an aeroplane at the age of 16 – before he could drive a car!

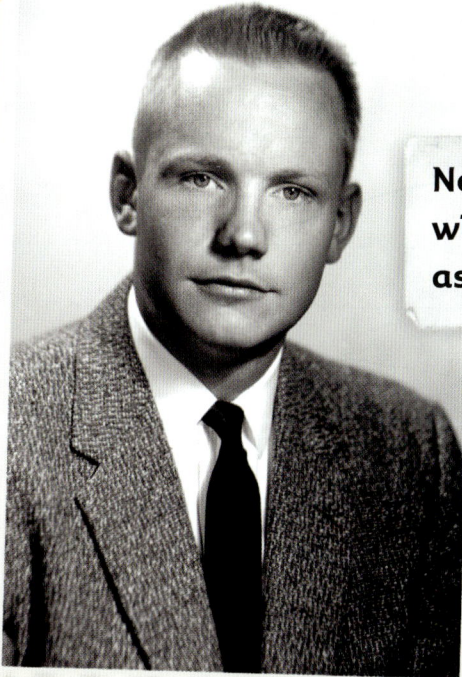

Neil as a young man, when he worked as a **test pilot**.

SENIORS

NEIL A. ARMSTRONG
"He thinks, he acts, 'tis done."

Band 2, 3, 4, Vice-President 4; Orchestra 3; Glee
Club 2; Student Council 3, 4, Vice-President 4;
Retrospect Staff; Junior Hi-Y 2; Senior Hi-Y 3, 4;
Boosters Club 2, 3, 4; Junior Class Play; Home Room
President 3; Boys' State 3; Transferred from Upper
Sandusky High School 1.

Neil's classmates wrote about him in his high school yearbook saying, "he thinks, he acts, 'tis done."

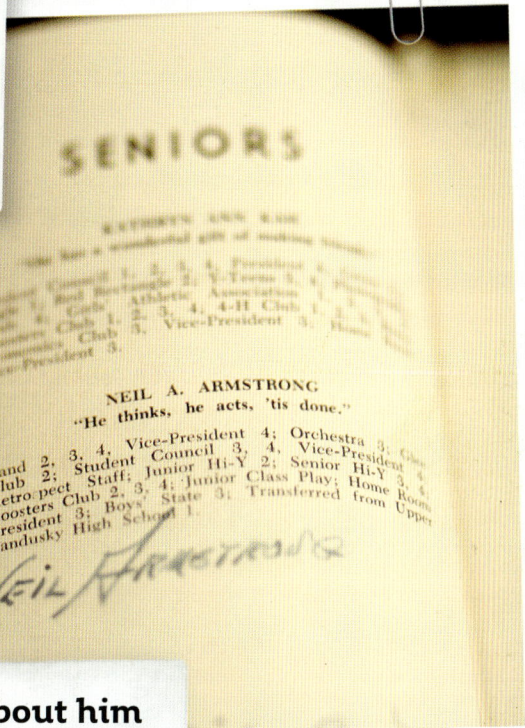

Becoming an explorer

Neil was a pilot in the US Navy and fought in the **Korean War**. Then he became a test pilot for fast jet planes. He was a very skilled **engineer** as well as a pilot, so he understood how the planes worked. He could also stay calm in difficult and dangerous situations. He was so good at these difficult jobs that **NASA** invited him to be an astronaut in 1962.

Neil in the cockpit of a rocket-powered X-15 plane after a test flight

Neil proved himself working as a pilot of extremely fast planes.

Walking on the moon

In 1969, Neil was in charge of a mission
to land on the moon. He travelled into
space with two other astronauts:
Buzz Aldrin and Michael Collins.

Neil and Buzz landed on the surface
of the moon in a **lunar module**,
and Neil became the first human
to set foot on the moon. Neil and Buzz
spent two hours on the moon,
collecting rocks and taking photos.

Down to Earth

Neil could look at the Earth from the moon
and cover it with his thumb – it was so far away!
But he said that this didn't make him feel like
a giant. Instead he felt very, very small.

Millions of people across the world watched on
television as Neil walked on the moon. When he
came back to Earth he was famous, but he didn't
like the attention. He didn't go on any more space
missions and instead became a teacher
at a university.

Neil (second from right) and the other Apollo 11 astronauts meet US President Nixon (far right).

What makes a great explorer?

Christopher Columbus was a great explorer because:

- He learnt the skills he needed to navigate.
- He was determined. It took years to find someone to pay for his ships.
- He was brave to sail across an unknown ocean.
- He was a good leader.

Neil Armstrong was a great explorer because:

- He studied engineering and understood how spacecraft worked.
- He was brave. He often faced danger in his work.
- He stayed calm and in control when things went wrong.
- He treated the mission to the moon seriously and didn't try to show off.

How we remember Columbus and Armstrong

We remember Christopher Columbus as a famous explorer who found new lands around the world. We know that he was skilled and courageous, but that he treated the islanders he met badly by stealing from them and using them as slaves.

Neil Armstrong will always be remembered as the first human to walk on the moon and for the words that he spoke as he stepped on it: "That's one small step for man, one giant leap for **mankind**."

Glossary

compass	tool that is used to show direction
engineer	person who designs or builds machinery or structures
Korean War	a war fought in the 1950s between North Korea and South Korea
licence	a permit to own or use something, or to do something in particular
lunar module	part of a spacecraft designed to land on the moon
mankind	the whole of the human race
merchant	person who buys and sells goods
NASA	National Aeronautics and Space Administration organisation that carries out space missions and research
navigated	found the right direction
port	harbour where ships are kept
test pilot	pilot who tries new types of aircraft
trade	buying and selling goods
voyage	sea journey

Christopher Columbus

around 1450	1492	1493	1498	1502	1506
born in Genoa	sails west and discovers the Americas	sails back to Spain and then back to the Americas	returns to the Americas	makes his final voyage to the Americas	returns to Spain and dies

Neil Armstrong

1930 **1946** **1949** **1969** **1971** **2012**

born in Ohio,
USA

gets
a pilot's licence

fights in
the Korean War

lands on
the moon

becomes
a university
teacher

dies

Ideas for reading

Written by Gillian Howell
Primary Literacy Consultant

Learning objectives: continue to apply phonic knowledge and skills as the route to decode words until automatic decoding has become embedded and reading is fluent; discussing the sequence of events in books and how items of information are related; being introduced to non-fiction books that are structured in different ways; participate in discussion about books, poems and other works that are read to them and those that they can read for themselves, taking turns and listening to what others say

Curriculum links: History; Geography

Interest words: incredible, Genoa, Asia, ocean, voyage, aeroplanes, licence, engineer, calm, situations, astronaut, mission, television, university, designs

Word Count: 795

Resources: pens and paper

Getting started

This book can be read over two or more reading sessions.

- Look together at the front cover and read the title. Ask the children what an explorer does.

- Turn to the back cover and read the blurb. Ask them what they already know about these two explorers and what they think they will find out by reading the book.

Reading and responding

- Read the chapter headings in the contents list and discuss what the children think the chapters will be about.

- Draw the children's attention to the glossary at the foot of the contents list. Ask them to say what the purpose of a glossary is and how it is used.

- Read pp2–3 to the children and discuss the illustrations. Ask them to suggest what is the same and what is different about the two explorers. Ask them to read to the end of the book and find out what it takes to be a great explorer.